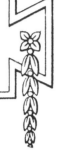

SCHIRMER'S LIBRARY
OF MUSICAL CLASSICS

JOHANN SEBASTIAN BACH

Two- and Three-Part Inventions

For the Piano

Edited and Fingered by
DR. WM. MASON

TWO-PART INVENTIONS
Library Vol. 379

→ **THREE-PART INVENTIONS**
Library Vol. 380

Complete — Library Vol. 16

G. SCHIRMER, Inc.

DISTRIBUTED BY
HAL•LEONARD®
CORPORATION
7777 W. BLUEMOUND RD. P.O. BOX 13819 MILWAUKEE, WI 53213

PREFACE

J. S. BACH appears to have written the 2-part and 3-part Inventions for his pupils expressly as a preparation for his larger works—more especially for the "Well-tempered Clavichord"—and for this purpose they cannot be too highly recommended. Even at the present day, assiduous practice of these Inventions will be of the utmost utility to each and every talented student of pianoforte-playing who wishes to rise above mediocrity, as regards developing his fingers and his musical taste. For in none of the recent, easier piano-pieces does the left-hand part contain such an independent treatment of the theme, as in these Inventions.

The title which Bach bestowed on these Inventions reads, literally:

"A faithful Guide, whereby admirers of the Clavichord are shewn a plain Method of learning not only to play clean in two Parts, but likewise in further Progress to manage three *obbligato* Parts well and correctly, and at the same time not merely how to get good *Inventions* [ideas], but also how to develop the same well; but above all, to obtain a *cantabile* Style of playing, and together with this to get a strong Foretaste of [the art of] Composition."

The keys common to both sets are C-major, C-minor, D-major, D-minor, Eb-major, E-major, E-minor, F-major, F-minor, G-major, G-minor, A-major, A-minor, Bb-major, B-minor. The 2-part Inventions were composed in Cöthen; those in 3-parts, on the other hand, were probably not finished until the beginning of the Leipzig period. Of the two original manuscripts of this work, one is in the "Clavierbüchlein für W. F. Bach" (Cöthen, 1720); the other, with numerous emendations, was formerly in the possession of Ph. E. Bach, and passed later into Louis Spohr's hands.

EMBELLISHMENTS

(*Les Agréments*)

For the convenience of students the embellishments are in this edition written out in full in smaller notes—the Mordent and Reversed Mordent or Praller being given for the most part in the text, while the manner of playing long or short trills, turns, or gruppettos and arpeggios is indicated in detail in the margin either above or below the embellishment-sign.

Composers of Bach's time were far from uniform in their use of these embellishments. A composer would, apparently without method, use many different signs to express the same thing—or the same sign for different things. In modern times many of the best authorities seem to agree that it accords with good musical taste to make the auxiliary or alternating lower tone of the Mordent conform to the key in which the piece is written. So also as regards the Reversed Mordent, or Praller, the auxiliary tone is the next diatonic degree above the principal.

The student must remember that the first note of these embellishments does not borrow its time from the preceding beat, but falls exactly upon its own part of the measure—or, otherwise expressed, it is simultaneous with its accompanying part, or parts, when such are present.

Both the Mordent and the Reversed Mordent may be played with two, or with three fingers in alternation. Both ways of fingering are indicated over or under the notes, but the latter way is much the better on many accounts, and is strongly recommended. Where two kinds of fingering are marked, the editor's preference is for the upper one.

Fifteen Three-Part Inventions.

Allegro moderato.

JOHANN SEBASTIAN BACH.

1.

Allegretto grazioso.

3.

dolce.

14

Allegro moderato.

6.

Andante espressivo.

Allegro moderato.

8.

mf leggiero.

Allegro moderato.

10.

Allegretto moderato.

11.

13.

Andante con moto.

14.

*) The crossing of hands here is extremely awkward. The notes may be more con-
veniently distributed between the hands in the following way, and, if played with pre-
cision, the effect of the contrary motion will be preserved.

EDITOR.